Body Needs

VITAMINS and MINERALS

for a healthy body

Heinemann Library
Chicago, Illinois

Angela Royston

Created by the publishing team at Heinemann Library
Designed by Ron Kamen and Celia Floyd
Illustrations by Geoff Ward
Originated by Ambassador Litho
Printed in China

07 06 05 04
10 9 8 7 6 5 4 3 2

Library of Congress Cataloging-in-Publication Data

Royston, Angela.
    Vitamins and minerals for a healthy body / Angela Royston.
        p. cm.
    Summary: Discusses what vitamins and minerals are, how they are digested, absorbed, and used by the body, and the role of these substances in a healthy diet.
    Includes bibliographical references and index.
    ISBN 1-40340-758-4 (lib. bdg.)
    ISBN 1-40343-3135 (pbk. bdg.)
    1. Vitamins in human nutrition--Juvenile literature.
2. Minerals
  in the body--Juvenile literature.   [1. Vitamins. 2. Minerals in
  nutrition. 3. Nutrition.]   I. Title. II. Series.
    QP771.R696 2003
    612.3'99--dc21

2002012645

Acknowledgments

The author and publishers are grateful to the following for permission to reproduce copyright material: pp. 4 (PPG International/Bill Losh), 7 (FPG International/VCL), 40 (FPG International/Gibson) Getty Images; p. 6 Photodisc; pp. 8, 9, 28 Liz Eddison; p. 10 Roger Scruton; pp. 14 (B. O. Veisland, MI&I), 15 (Eye of Science), 17 (Prof. P. Motta/ Department of Anatomy/University La Sapienza, Rome), 21 (Mark Clarke), 34 (Jim Varney), 35 (Biophoto Associates), 37 (John Paul Kay, Peter Arnold Inc.), 41 (Bettina Salomon) SPL; pp. 16, 19, 20, 23, 27, 30 Gareth Boden; pp. 31, 32 (Paul Barton), 33, 36 Corbis.

Cover photograph of a strawberry and cream, reproduced with permission of Getty/Foodpix.

Every effort has been made to contact copyright holders of any material reproduced in this book. Any omissions will be rectified in subsequent printings if notice is given to the publisher.

Some words are shown in bold, **like this.** You can find out what they mean by looking in the glossary.

Contents

Fueling the Body Machine

Your body works like a very complicated machine. Most machines involve electrical wiring, screws, and bolts, but the body uses chemicals and **chemical reactions** instead. In fact, most of the body's functions rely on different chemical reactions. Your body makes some of the chemicals itself, but it has to take in all the rest from the outside world. It gets **oxygen** from the air and a wide range of chemicals from food. The chemicals that come from food are called **nutrients.**

Nutrients

The main nutrients in food are **carbohydrates, fats,** and **proteins.** They supply your body with **energy** and the chemicals it needs to grow and replace **cells.** In addition to the main nutrients, your body needs small amounts of vitamins and minerals to help it carry out all the chemical processes that make it work. This book is about vitamins and minerals. But since most foods contain a mixture of different kinds of nutrients, we will take a look at the other nutrients first.

Carbohydrates

Foods such as bread, potatoes, pasta, and rice contain lots of carbohydrates in the form of **starch.** The body changes the starch into **glucose,** or sugar, which the muscles and other parts of your body use for energy. Sugar and foods that contain a lot of natural sugar, such as fruits, are also rich in carbohydrates.

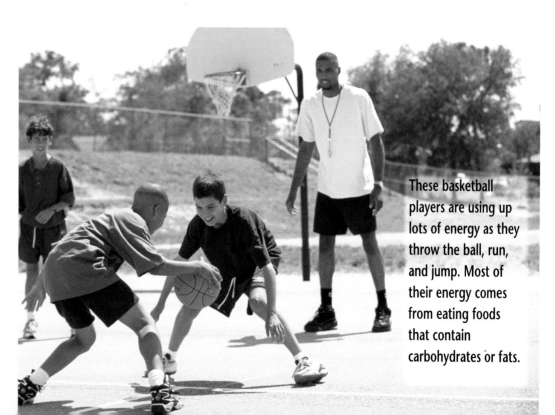

These basketball players are using up lots of energy as they throw the ball, run, and jump. Most of their energy comes from eating foods that contain carbohydrates or fats.

4

Fats

Fats also supply the body with energy, but in a more concentrated form than carbohydrates. If your body gets more carbohydrates and fats than it needs, it stores the extra as a layer of fat under your skin and around **organs**, such as your heart.

Protein

Your body is made of millions of tiny cells. Different kinds of cells make up your skin, muscles, and bones. Some cells do not last long before they have to be replaced. Cells consist mainly of water and protein. Your body uses proteins that you get from foods such as meat, fish, eggs, beans, and cheese to build new cells. It is particularly important that children eat plenty of protein, because they are still growing and their bodies need to make millions of extra cells.

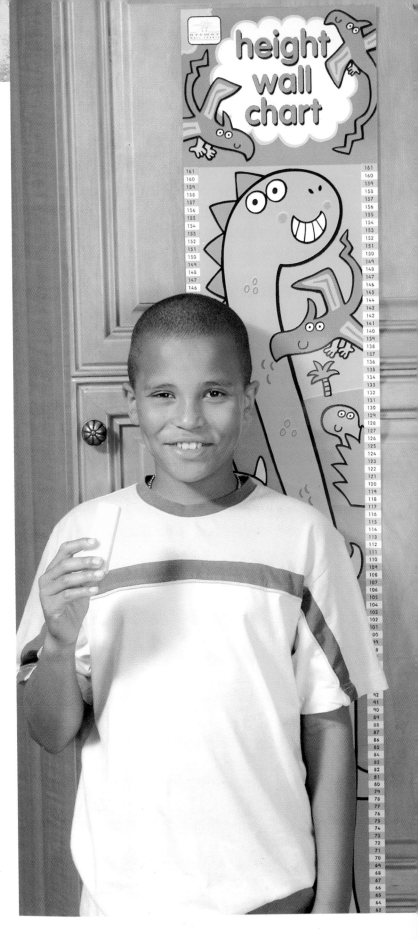

This boy's height will be measured to see how tall he has grown. The protein in the cheese he is eating will help him keep on growing.

Vitamins and Minerals

Most food consists of water and one of the main **nutrients: carbohydrates, fats,** or **proteins.** But food also contains small amounts of vitamins and minerals. The fact that they only contain small amounts is fine, because your body only needs tiny amounts of each to stay healthy. The amounts are so small that most are measured as thousandth parts of a gram (milligram, or mg) or hundredth parts of a gram (centigram, or cg). Still, without vitamins and minerals you would soon get ill.

Too small to find

Vitamins and minerals are needed in such small amounts that for hundreds of years scientists did not know that most existed. They knew that to be healthy and to grow well, people needed to eat fats, proteins, carbohydrates, and some minerals. Since 1753, they had also known about the importance of fruit. Before then, sailors on long voyages often died of scurvy. Scurvy is a disease that keeps wounds from healing well and causes blood to leak from the tiny blood vessels under the skin and in the gums. A ship's doctor, James Lind, thought that the sailors' diet, which did not include fruits or vegetables, might be causing the scurvy. He tried adding various foods, but the scurvy only stopped when he gave the sailors lemons and oranges.

Discovery of vitamins

About 150 years later, in 1906, the scientist Frederick Hopkins experimented with the diet of rats. He discovered that "astonishingly small amounts" of some substances are needed for the body to be able to use the main nutrients. Since then, scientists have learned a lot about how the body uses both vitamins and minerals. Some are needed by all the **cells** in the body, while others, such as the vitamin C in lemon juice, work only in certain kinds of cells. Vitamin C is needed to build strong blood vessels and to help wounds heal. This book is about the different vitamins and minerals and what happens if you eat too much or too little of them.

Lemons are a good source of vitamin C.

Minerals in the Body

Calcium is the most common mineral in the body. About one percent of your weight is calcium. So if you weigh 65 pounds (30 kilograms), you have about 11 ounces (300 grams) of calcium in your body. There is much less of other minerals. Most adults, for example, have only about 0.11 to 0.14 ounces (3 to 4 grams) of iron in their bodies.

Many foods contain small amounts of a few vitamins and minerals, so you need to eat a wide variety of food, especially vegetables and fruits, to get them all. The food in this shopping cart will keep a whole family well supplied with vitamins and minerals for a week.

What Are Vitamins?

Vitamins are chemical mixtures that contain carbon and various other chemicals and that are found in plants and animals. We need thirteen different vitamins to help our bodies carry out all the processes needed to stay alive. You can make five of these vitamins in your body, but the rest you have to get from the food you eat.

Identifying vitamins

Vitamins are sometimes known by their chemical names but are often identified by a letter of the alphabet. For example, thiamine is often known as vitamin B_1 and ascorbic acid as vitamin C. Vitamins A, D, E, and K **dissolve** in **fat** and are carried into the body mainly in fatty or oily food. The rest, the B vitamins and vitamin C, can dissolve in water.

Vitamin A

The chemical name of vitamin A is retinol. Retinol itself is only found in animal foods, particularly liver and cod-liver oil. But many fruits and vegetables contain carotenes, which are yellow, red, or orange substances. Carotenes can be converted in the body to retinal. The most important carotene is beta-carotene, which is found in carrots, red peppers, sweet potatoes, spinach, and mangoes.

Most vitamins are found in a variety of foods. The foods here contain vitamins A, D, E, and K, the vitamins that are **soluble** in fat.

8

Vitamin C and the B vitamins are soluble in water. These foods are rich in either the B vitamins or vitamin C. Some even have both.

B vitamins

Several different vitamins are included in a group called the B vitamins. They are grouped together because of the way the body uses them, but many are also found in the same foods. Milk, meat, cereal, bread, and potatoes are good sources of several of the B vitamins. Vitamin B_{12} is more difficult to get. It is found only in food that comes from animals, such as meat, fish, eggs, cheese, and milk.

Vitamin C

Vitamin C is found mainly in plants, including potatoes. In fact, the only plants that do not contain vitamin C are grains, dried peas, and dried beans. You get much more vitamin C from eating fresh, raw fruits and vegetables than from cooked ones, since vitamin C is easily destroyed when it is heated or stored.

Making vitamins in the body

Although vitamins D and K are found in various foods, your body can make them itself. Vitamin D is sometimes called the "sunshine vitamin," because when your skin is exposed to sunlight, the vitamin forms in your skin. You get some vitamin K from spinach, cabbage, cauliflower, peas, and grains. Vitamin K is also made inside your body by **bacteria** in the large intestine.

What Are Minerals?

Minerals are **elements** that are found in the ground. They include iron, zinc, copper, and other metals that are used to make things. But living things need minerals, too, although only in small amounts. Living things cannot make minerals and so have to take them in from the outside world. Your body needs about fifteen minerals to function and grow healthy. Some of these are particularly important and are called the major minerals. They are calcium, phosphorus, potassium, sodium, magnesium, iron, and zinc.

These nails are made mainly of iron. The mineral that makes up this metal is needed by your body to help it work properly.

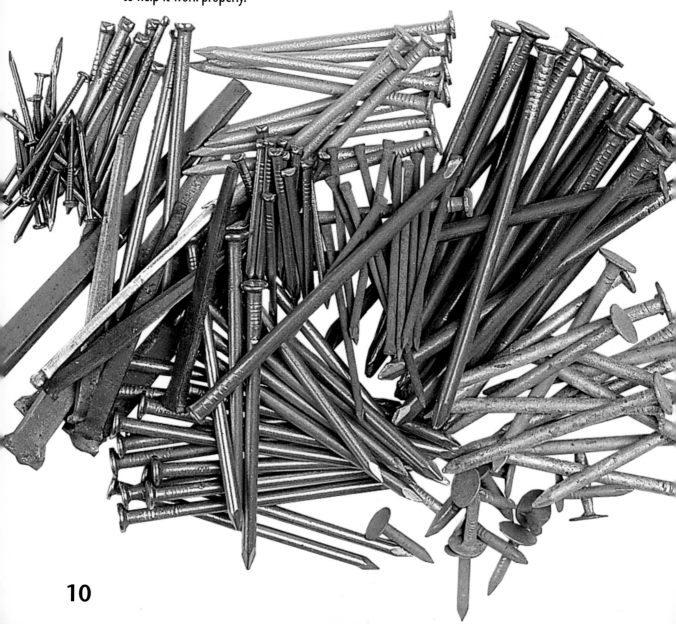

Trace Elements

In addition to the major minerals, your body needs tiny amounts of seven other minerals, including copper, chromium, fluoride, and iodine. We call these the **trace elements**. Other than fluoride, these minerals are available in common foods. Fluoride makes teeth stronger and is added to most toothpastes and to some sources of tap water.

How we get minerals

Small amounts of minerals are scattered through the soil and some **dissolve** in water. Plants take in the water with the dissolved minerals in it through their roots. The minerals are taken to all parts of the plant and are then passed on to any animals that eat them, so most of our food contains some minerals. Milk, meat, vegetables, and bread and other foods made from grains are richest in the major minerals.

Milk and meat

Milk and dairy products such as cheese and yogurt contain all the major minerals, although they are not a very good source of iron. Milk and cheese are especially rich in calcium, the mineral needed for strong bones and teeth. Meat, particularly liver, is the best source of iron, although other foods such as sardines, some breakfast cereals, and chocolate contain iron, too.

Bread, other grains, and plants

Bread and other grain-based food, such as pasta and rice, contain all the major minerals, although they have less potassium than other minerals. Bananas and other fruits and vegetables are good sources of potassium. Some vegetables are particularly rich in certain minerals. Spinach and winter squash, for example, contain both calcium and iron, while potatoes are rich in magnesium and potassium.

Salt

Table salt is made up of two elements, sodium and chlorine, combined together. Salt is naturally present in most foods, while some foods, such as bacon, potato chips, soy sauce, and canned soups, have a lot of salt added to them. In addition, many people add salt to the food they eat, although their normal diet contains plenty of salt already.

Digesting Vitamins and Minerals

Food contains the vitamins and minerals you need, but it has to be digested before your body can use them. The process of digestion breaks up food into smaller and smaller pieces. Digestion begins in your mouth and continues in your stomach and small intestine. Special chemicals called **enzymes** help break down **carbohydrates, fats,** and **proteins.** Vitamins and minerals do not need to be broken down but are taken into the blood with water or fats.

In the mouth

As you chew food, your teeth mash it up and mix it with **saliva** until it forms a soft, mushy lump. Then your tongue pushes it to the back of your mouth and you swallow it. It passes down your throat, through your **pharynx** into your **esophagus,** and then into your stomach.

In the stomach

Your stomach is sort of like a food blender. It churns the food around and mixes it with digestive juices made in the wall of the stomach. The food slowly turns into a kind of thick soup, called **chyme.** From the stomach, chyme passes to the small intestine, where the next stage of digestion occurs.

In the duodenum

The first part of the small intestine is called the **duodenum.** It is about 12 inches (30 centimeters) long. It is supplied with **bile** from the gall bladder and digestive juices from the walls of the small intestine and from the pancreas. Bile is made in the **liver** and stored in the gall bladder. It acts on fats in the same way as dishwashing liquid does. Bile breaks fats up into tiny droplets so that it can be digested.

The rest of the small intestine

As the chyme passes through the small intestine it is swirled backward and forward. This helps the digestive juices mix with the chyme and get to work. Digestive juices contain enzymes that the body makes to break fats, carbohydrates, and proteins into smaller units. Fats take the longest to break up. It is not until they reach the end of the small intestine that most are absorbed into the blood.

Stomach Facts

Your stomach stretches as it fills up with food. How long the food stays in the stomach depends on what it is and how much there is of it. On average, food stays in your stomach for about two to three hours.

This is a diagram of the digestive system.

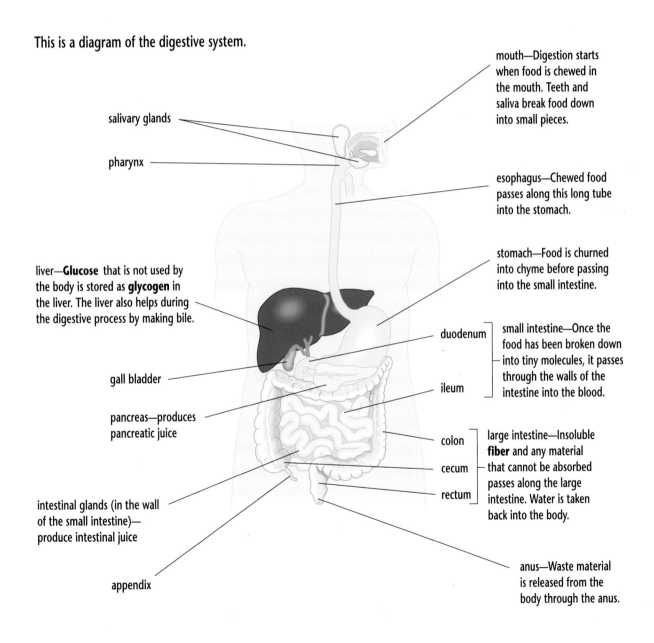

mouth—Digestion starts when food is chewed in the mouth. Teeth and saliva break food down into small pieces.

salivary glands

pharynx

esophagus—Chewed food passes along this long tube into the stomach.

stomach—Food is churned into chyme before passing into the small intestine.

liver—**Glucose** that is not used by the body is stored as **glycogen** in the liver. The liver also helps during the digestive process by making bile.

duodenum

small intestine—Once the food has been broken down into tiny molecules, it passes through the walls of the intestine into the blood.

gall bladder

ileum

pancreas—produces pancreatic juice

colon

cecum

large intestine—Insoluble **fiber** and any material that cannot be absorbed passes along the large intestine. Water is taken back into the body.

rectum

intestinal glands (in the wall of the small intestine)— produce intestinal juice

anus—Waste material is released from the body through the anus.

appendix

Absorbing Vitamins and Minerals

When **carbohydrates, fats,** and **proteins** have been broken down into small enough pieces, they are ready to be absorbed into the blood. Most **nutrients,** including minerals and vitamins, are absorbed through the walls of the stomach and small intestine. Some nutrients pass through the **liver,** which returns them to the blood for the rest of the body to use.

The villi

The inside lining of the small intestine is covered with millions of tiny, fingerlike extensions called **villi.** The villi even have smaller microvilli covering them. Villi increase the surface area of the small intestine. Surface area is the space occupied by the surface of something. It is easy to measure if something is flat, like a table. But to find out the surface area of the small intestine, the folded tube would have to be straightened out and each villi would have to be flattened. This is why the surface area of the small intestine is so much bigger than it first seems.

Absorbing water

As food is broken down, the water in it is squeezed out. Water passes easily through the walls of the villi into the blood and carries with it whatever is **dissolved** in it. Minerals, vitamin C, and some of the B vitamins are absorbed in the **duodenum,** the first part of the small intestine. More B vitamins are absorbed in the rest of the small intestine.

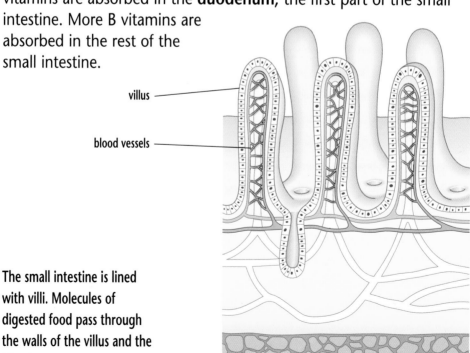

villus

blood vessels

The small intestine is lined with villi. Molecules of digested food pass through the walls of the villus and the blood vessels into the blood.

Absorbing fat-soluble vitamins

Bile breaks up fats into tiny droplets, which are then digested by **enzymes**. They break the large fat molecules into smaller units, called **fatty acids**. As the fatty acids are absorbed into the blood, the vitamins dissolved in them are absorbed, too.

Not all vitamins and minerals are absorbed

Some vitamins and minerals are dependent on other factors being present in order for them to be absorbed. For example, vitamin B_6 is needed for zinc to be absorbed, and vitamin C helps iron to be absorbed. Some foods, such as tea, coffee, rhubarb, and wheat, contain substances that make it less likely that iron or other nutrients will be absorbed.

The large intestine

Anything that is not absorbed in the small intestine passes through to the large intestine. Here millions of **bacteria** help to process the waste material. While this is happening, the bacteria make vitamin K, which passes into the blood. At the same time, water passes from the undigested mush into the blood. The waste food (mixed with digestive juices, bacteria, and other waste matter) slowly becomes more solid. This solid waste, or feces, is pushed out of the body through the anus.

This photo shows what bacteria in the large intestine look like under a microscope.

How the Body Uses Vitamins

Vitamins are needed by all the millions of **cells** in the body and are necessary for them to work properly. Most vitamins perform several different jobs. Most do some work in all cells, but some vitamins work only in certain kinds of cells. For example, folate, one of the B vitamins, is used in the **bone marrow** to produce new red blood cells.

Helping cells

Vitamins form part of many **enzymes.** This means that they are needed for **chemical reactions** to take place, but they are not part of the reaction itself. The main **nutrients** in food give your body **energy** and the materials to build new cells. But your body cannot use the main nutrients without the help of vitamins and minerals. They allow the cells to change **fats** and sugar from **carbohydrates** into energy. Others help the cells use **proteins** to build new cells and repair other cells.

Protecting against cancer

Some vitamins help prevent **free-radical** damage that can lead to cancer. As the body carries out its normal chemical reactions, it makes chemicals called free radicals. Free radicals can damage protein and **DNA** in the body's cells. DNA is the **molecule** that contains your **genetic code** and tells your body how to build and repair itself. If the cells cannot repair the damage, they may become cancer cells. Vitamins C and E and some beta-carotenes fight these dangerous free radicals.

This girl is making herself a snack that is rich in carbohydrates, but her body cannot turn the carbohydrates into energy without the help of vitamins.

Preventing heart disease

Eating a good amount of fruits and vegetables daily may be prevent certain diseases such as heart disease. **Cholesterol** can build up in the blood vessels of the heart and cause the vessels to narrow. Fruits and vegetables contain important vitamins and minerals and other substances that act as **antioxidants.** These antioxidants help prevent the vessels in the heart from becoming narrow.

Vitamin A

Vitamin A makes your skin, hair, and nails healthy, but it does not work if you rub it into your hair or skin. Vitamins only work as part of a diet from inside the body. Vitamin A also helps children grow well. It does this because the body needs it to produce new cells.

Seeing in the Dark

Carrots really do help you see in the dark. This is because they are rich in vitamin A. The cells in your eyes need vitamin A to help them make the most of dim light. Without it, you would not be able to see anything at night.

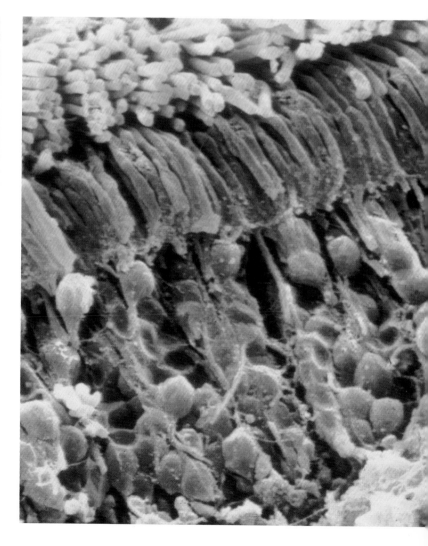

This is what the cells in your eyes that react to dim light look like under a microscope. The purple color is due to vitamin A. When light hits these cells, the purple changes to white and this chemical change triggers the nerves that allow you to see.

17

Using B Vitamins and Vitamin C

Both B vitamins and vitamin C are **soluble** in water. You need a constant supply of them, because your body cannot store them. Some B vitamins help your **cells** change food into **energy,** while others build new **proteins.** Vitamin C helps keep your skin, bones, and other tissues healthy.

Releasing energy from food

The B vitamins thiamine (B_1), riboflavin (B_2), and niacin are all needed by the cells to release energy from food. Thiamine works only on **carbohydrates,** while riboflavin helps to release the energy in **fats** and proteins as well as carbohydrates. Two more B vitamins—pantothenic acid and biotin—are needed for your body to use the energy in fats.

Using protein

During digestion, protein in your food is broken down into units called **amino acids.** Vitamin B_6 helps your cells rebuild the amino acids into new proteins. One of these proteins is **hemoglobin,** the substance that makes red blood cells red. Hemoglobin takes in **oxygen** from the air you breathe in and carries it to the rest of the body. Vitamin B_6 can also make the B vitamin niacin from one of the amino acids.

Vitamin B_{12} and folate

Vitamin B_{12} and folate are needed in parts of the body where cells are being made very quickly. For example, your **bone marrow**—the soft jelly-like substance in the middle of some bones—makes about 100 million new red blood cells every minute. It cannot do this without vitamin B_{12} and folate. Both of these vitamins also help form healthy nerve cells.

Cook Your Eggs

Egg yolks contain the B vitamin biotin, but your body can only use it if the egg is cooked. Otherwise a substance contained in raw egg white combines with biotin and prevents the body from using it.

Connective tissue

Vitamin C is needed to produce collagen, the substance that forms the structure of your skin, bones, teeth, and connective tissue. Connective tissue is strong but stretchy. It keeps your heart, lungs, and stomach in place, but allows them to move as you bend, twist, and stretch. Other examples of connective tissue include gums, which hold your teeth in your jaws; tendons, which attach your muscles to your bones; and ligaments, which hold your joints together.

Other uses of vitamin C

Vitamin C builds strong blood vessels and helps wounds heal. Vitamin C also helps your body absorb iron from foods other than meat.

Oranges, strawberries, and cantaloupe are just some of the fruits that are particularly rich in vitamin C. Eating them will help to keep this girl's gums, teeth, and other tissues healthy.

Using Vitamins D, E, and K

Vitamins D, E, and K, like vitamin A, are all **soluble** in **fat.** This means that the body can store them. Each one has a certain job to do in the body.

Vitamin D

The main task of vitamin D is to help your body absorb the mineral calcium. Much of the vitamin D in your body is made by sunlight acting on your skin, but if you usually keep your skin covered, you may need to get the vitamin from food. The **liver** and the kidneys process vitamin D. They turn it into a substance that controls the amount of calcium that is absorbed into the blood through your digestive system.

Calcium in the bones

Calcium also needs vitamin D after it has been absorbed into the blood. Most of the calcium you eat is deposited in your bones and teeth, where it makes them strong. Scientists think that you need vitamin D for your bones and teeth to take in the calcium.

This girl is getting vitamin D from two sources—from the yogurt she is eating and from sunlight on her skin. Vitamin D will help the calcium in the yogurt form strong bones and teeth.

Vitamin E

Vitamin E is important in the body because it acts as an **antioxidant**. This means that it helps to prevent damage by the chemicals called **free radicals** that can cause cancer and heart disease. Vitamin E also has several other functions. These functions include helping to keep normal cell structure. It is also needed by the body's immune system to keep the body healthy.

Vitamin K

Vitamin K helps blood clot and wounds heal. If you cut yourself, blood flows from the tiny blood vessels in your skin. Several chemicals make the blood in the wound become thicker and form a clot. The clot hardens to form a scab, which protects the wound while the blood vessels heal and new skin grows.

Blood Facts
Blood can carry the **bacteria** and **viruses** that cause serious diseases. If you help someone clean or bandage a cut, do not let his or her blood touch your skin or get inside your body. Always cover cuts with a clean bandage.

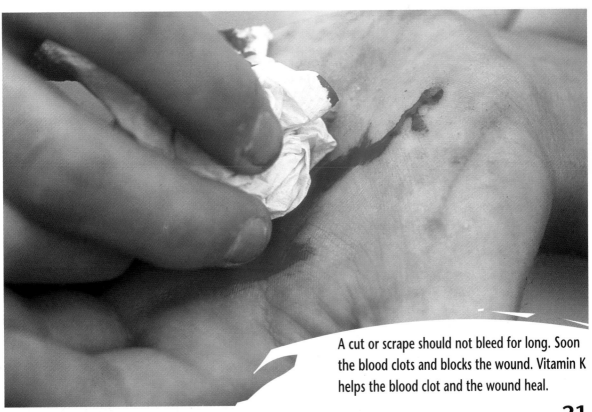

A cut or scrape should not bleed for long. Soon the blood clots and blocks the wound. Vitamin K helps the blood clot and the wound heal.

How the Body Uses Minerals

Minerals are used throughout the body, both inside and outside the **cells.** They have three main functions. Some make your bones and teeth strong. Others become part of your cells and bodily fluids such as blood and sweat. The rest are needed to make **enzymes,** the substances that help your cells carry out **chemical reactions.**

Bones

The minerals that make bones and teeth hard are calcium, phosphorus, and magnesium. Your bones use 99 percent of the calcium, 75 percent of the phosphorus, and half of the magnesium in your body. Without them, your bones would still be strong, but they would be bendy like cartilage—the substance that you can feel at the tips of your ears.

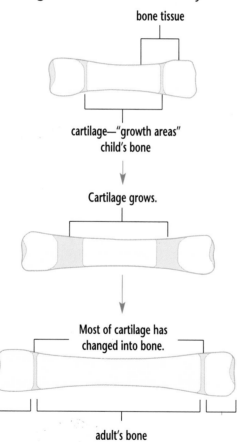

bone tissue

cartilage—"growth areas"
child's bone

Cartilage grows.

Most of cartilage has
changed into bone.

adult's bone

A child's bone contains much more cartilage than an adult's bone. As the cartilage absorbs minerals and changes into bone, the child's bone slowly grows and new cartilage forms at the ends.

Calcium storage

Calcium can move in and out of your bones if it is needed elsewhere. Muscles work by contracting, that is, by getting shorter, but they need calcium to be able to do this. Your heart is a muscle, and it needs calcium, too. Bones act as a storage area for calcium in case your body is not getting enough from food.

Absorbing calcium

Your body absorbs less than half the amount of calcium your food contains. Several things can reduce this amount even more. You need vitamin D in order to absorb calcium and deposit it in your bones. If you are lacking in vitamin D, you will absorb less calcium. Some foods, especially spinach and rhubarb, contain chemicals that stop calcium from being absorbed into the blood. This does not mean that you should never eat spinach and rhubarb. It means that you should eat calcium-rich food separately.

Fluoride

Fluoride is a **trace element** that makes your teeth less likely to decay. **Bacteria** in your mouth feed on sugar and produce a strong **acid** that **dissolves** enamel, the hard coating on your teeth. Once the acid has made a hole (cavity) in the enamel of a tooth, it can eat its way through the **dentin** below, causing your tooth to rot. Fluoride works best on your teeth while they are still forming. Your baby teeth form before you are born, but your adult teeth are slowly forming until you are about ten years old.

Using toothpaste that contains fluoride helps keep your teeth from decaying.

Dissolving Bone
If you put a chicken bone in some vinegar (an acid) and leave it, the acid will slowly remove the calcium from the bone. After a few weeks the bone will have become bendy, like the cartilage it formed from.

Minerals in Bodily Fluids

Your body is full of liquids. In addition to your blood, sweat, tears, and other bodily fluids, every **cell** contains liquid. These liquids are mainly water with minerals and other substances **dissolved** in them. Minerals in the water inside and outside your cells control what passes into and out of the cells. Salt, containing the **elements** sodium and chlorine, helps to control the amount of water in your body.

Salt in the body

All your bodily fluids, including blood, urine, tears, and sweat, contain salt. The amounts of salt and other minerals in your body are controlled by your kidneys. They make sure that the concentration of salt in your blood stays about the same. If your blood contains extra salt, you will feel thirsty and drink extra water. If you eat very salty chips, for example, you will become thirsty. If your blood is low in salt, your kidneys get rid of extra water to keep the concentration of salt about the same.

Water and Sports

If you exercise or play sports, you have no doubt noticed yourself sweating during the activity. It is important that you replace the water that you lose through your skin when you exercise. The best way to do that is to drink plenty of water before, during, and after exercising. Do not wait until you are thirsty to get a drink. By that time, your body has already needed liquids for a while.

Sweat

If you lick your skin when you have been sweating, it will taste salty. Sweating helps control the temperature of the body. When you sweat your body loses water and minerals, especially salt. If the weather is very hot, or if you have been exercising very hard, you should drink extra water and eat a bit more salt to make up for what you have lost as sweat.

Border crossing

Blood carries the **nutrients** from digested food to all your cells. Each cell is surrounded by salty water. The liquid inside each cell contains potassium, magnesium, and phosphorus. These liquids allow nutrients and **oxygen** to pass from the blood into the cell. It also allows waste chemicals, such as **proteins** and **carbon dioxide** to pass from the cell into the blood. The blood carries the waste away so it can be removed from the body.

Body Fact

About two-thirds of your body is water. In an adult, this includes about 4 quarts (4.5 liters) of blood, 2.75 quarts (3 liters) of digestive juices, and about 8.5 ounces (250 milliliters) of urine.
The rest is liquid in and around the cells and tubes inside your body.

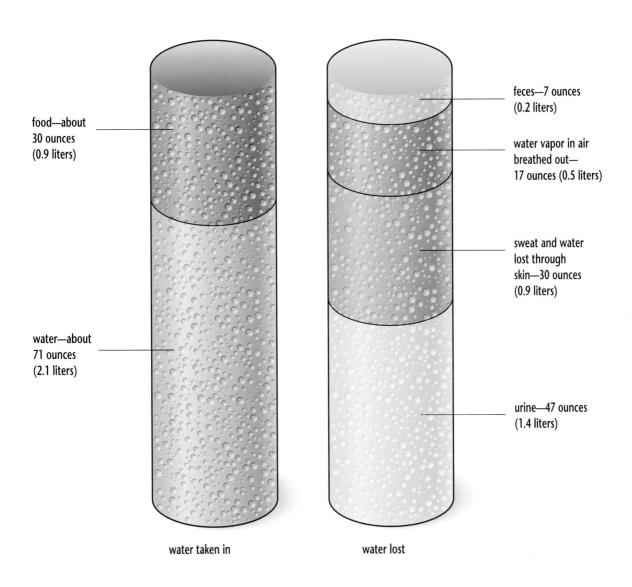

food—about
30 ounces
(0.9 liters)

water—about
71 ounces
(2.1 liters)

water taken in

feces—7 ounces
(0.2 liters)

water vapor in air
breathed out—
17 ounces (0.5 liters)

sweat and water
lost through
skin—30 ounces
(0.9 liters)

urine—47 ounces
(1.4 liters)

water lost

Your body takes in and loses water every day.
Salt in the body helps keep a balance between
the water you take in and the water you lose.

Minerals in Enzymes

Minerals and some vitamins form part of many **enzymes.** We have already seen how enzymes work in the digestive system, but enzymes also act inside every single body **cell.** One cell may have hundreds of small **chemical reactions** going on at the same time, each using a different enzyme. Enzymes speed up the rate at which chemicals react, and cells would not be able to stay alive without them.

Taking in oxygen

More than half the iron in your body is in your blood. It is contained in **hemoglobin,** the red substance in red blood cells. As blood passes through the lungs, **oxygen** from the air you breathe in becomes attached to hemoglobin. Later, as the blood is pumped around the body, the oxygen leaves the hemoglobin and passes into the cells.

Losing carbon dioxide

Oxygen combines with sugar to produce **energy** inside the cell. As it does so, **carbon dioxide** is produced. This gas passes out of the cell and attaches itself to hemoglobin that has lost its oxygen. The carbon dioxide leaves the blood in the lungs and is breathed out.

All the living cells in your body need to take in oxygen and get rid of waste (carbon dioxide). Red blood cells, which contain iron, move oxygen from the lungs to the cells and return carbon dioxide to the lungs.

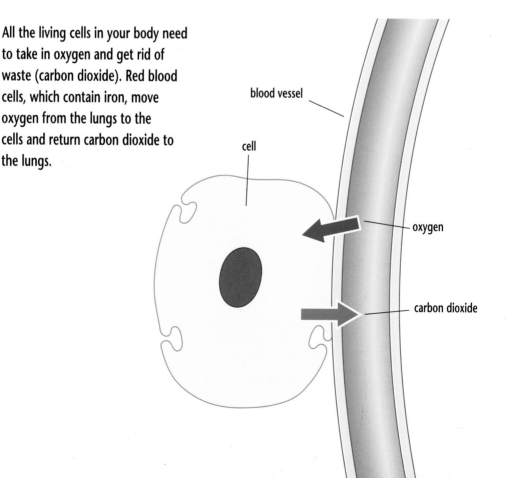

blood vessel

cell

oxygen

carbon dioxide

Iron in the body

What happens to the rest of the iron in your body? Some of it is used by the muscles, and the rest is stored in your **liver.** Other animals store iron in their liver, too. Eating chicken or beef liver is a good way to get iron into your own body. When red blood cells die, the iron in the hemoglobin is reused, so your body loses iron only when you lose blood. Iron is not easily absorbed into the body and needs vitamin C for even a quarter of the iron in food to pass into the blood.

Zinc

Zinc, like iron, is a major mineral. It works with many different enzymes. It is needed for children to grow and for their bodies to become mature at **puberty.** In addition, zinc helps wounds heal.

Trace elements

Most of the minerals known as **trace elements** (fluoride, copper, selenium, manganese, chromium, and cobalt), are used mainly by different enzymes. Iodine forms a part of the **hormones** produced by the **thyroid gland.** These hormones control your metabolic rate. That rate measures how fast your body changes food into energy, new cells, and waste materials.

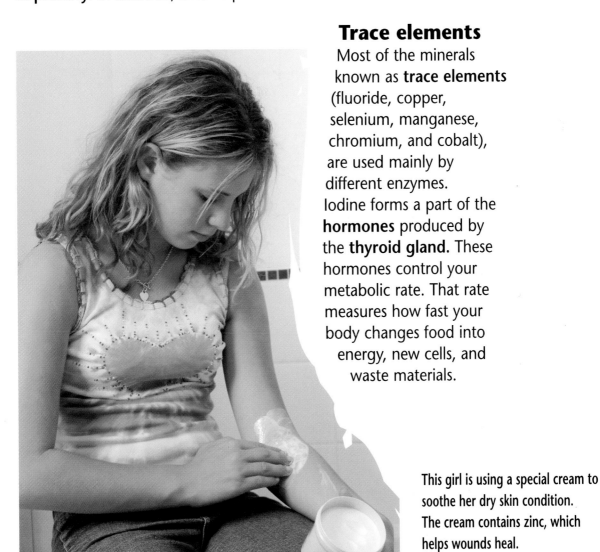

This girl is using a special cream to soothe her dry skin condition. The cream contains zinc, which helps wounds heal.

Too Much of a Good Thing

Your body needs so little of each vitamin and mineral that swallowing vitamin and mineral pills can give your body much more than it needs. Too much of some vitamins and minerals can harm you.

Supplements

Many vitamins and mineral pills are sold as cures for various conditions or simply to make you extra healthy. Most people will get all the vitamins and minerals they need by eating a wide variety of nutritious foods. In some cases, however, pills can be useful.

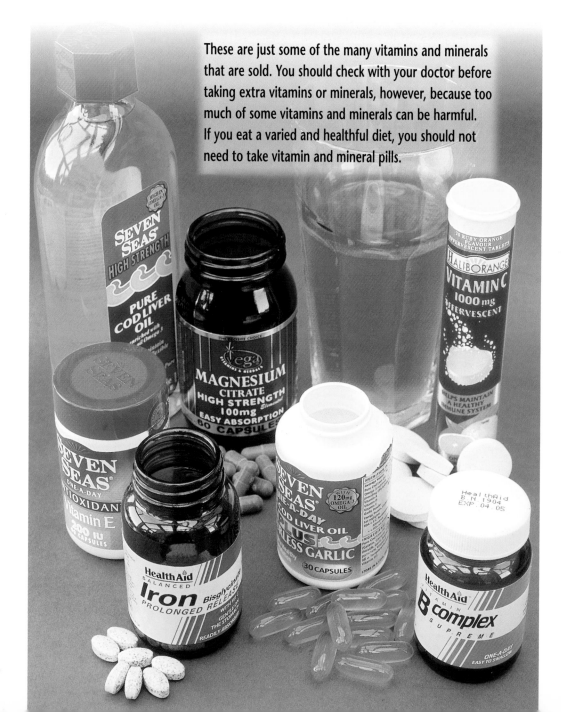

These are just some of the many vitamins and minerals that are sold. You should check with your doctor before taking extra vitamins or minerals, however, because too much of some vitamins and minerals can be harmful. If you eat a varied and healthful diet, you should not need to take vitamin and mineral pills.

Water-soluble vitamins

It does not matter if you have too much vitamin C or most B vitamins. They are **soluble** in water, and any extra is just filtered by your kidneys into your urine. There are a few exceptions to this, however. If you take too much niacin, one of the B vitamins, it can make your face and hands feel as if they are burning. It could even damage your **liver.** Too much Vitamin B$_6$ can harm your sensory nerves—the nerves that carry signals to your brain from your senses.

Fat-soluble vitamins

If you get more fat-soluble vitamins than your body needs, your liver stores the extra. This means that if your diet is short of vitamins A, D, E, or K for a short time, your body will simply use the supplies from the liver. Getting much too much of vitamins E or K does not harm you, but too much of vitamins A or D can.

Too much vitamin A

If you get too much vitamin A, the extra amount can poison your liver. Unborn babies are most at risk of being harmed by too much vitamin A. Pregnant women should avoid eating liver or things made of liver, such as liverwurst, because the large amount of vitamin A in liver may cause **birth defects** in their babies.

Too much vitamin D

Vitamin D controls how much calcium is absorbed into the body, so too much vitamin D can lead to problems. Extra calcium is usually filtered out in your urine, but, if there is more than your kidneys can deal with, the extra can damage them. Young children, in particular, should not add too much vitamin D to their diets.

Too Much Salt and Other Minerals

If you eat a balanced diet you will get enough—but not too much—of most minerals. However, many people eat more sodium (from salt) than they need, and this causes health problems for some people. Babies are especially at risk from too much sodium or phosphorus. Another common problem is too much fluoride, which can discolor teeth.

Added salt

There is enough natural salt in food to meet our needs, but salt makes food tastier and it is usually added when food is cooked. In addition, we often sprinkle more salt on to the food on our plates. Scientists figure that, on average, most people eat twice the amount of salt they need and some eat even more.

High blood pressure

If your blood contains extra salt, your kidneys filter out much of the extra amount. But the kidneys also keep extra water in the blood to balance the extra salt. This increases the volume of blood in your body and can cause high blood pressure. Blood pressure measures the force with which the heart pumps blood into the **arteries.** High blood pressure can damage the heart, cause **strokes,** and damage the kidneys. Children who eat too much salt are more likely to suffer from high blood pressure when they are older.

This package of chips contains about 0.014 ounces (385 milligrams) of sodium, or about a quarter of all the salt needed in a day. Peanuts and other salty snacks, bacon, and many packaged foods are very high in salt.

Mercury in Fish

Certain factories release mercury into the air. The mercury falls back to the ground and into bodies of water, contaminating fish. Mercury can damage an unborn child's nervous system, so the U.S. Food and Drug Administration recommends that pregnant women not eat certain types of fish.

Babies

A baby's kidneys cannot get rid of extra salt, which can damage their kidneys. Extra salt should never be added to a baby's food until the baby is at least a year old. There is enough natural salt in food to supply babies with all the sodium and chlorine they need. Newborn babies must be fed on breast milk or special formula milk, because plain cow's milk contains too much phosphorus for them.

Too much fluoride

Extra fluoride makes your teeth strong and less likely to need fillings, but some children get more fluoride than they need. Most brands of toothpaste contain fluoride. In some places, fluoride is added to tap water as well. You should not take fluoride pills if fluoride is added to the drinking water. Extra fluoride will make your teeth extra strong, but it may change their color.

Fluoride is added to some drinking water. Too much of it can discolor your teeth.

Deficiency Diseases

Eating a balanced and varied diet gives your body all the vitamins and minerals you need. However, people who do not get enough of just one of these necessary **nutrients** can suffer from a variety of problems. A shortage of a particular vitamin or mineral can cause one of many **deficiency diseases**.

Who suffers from deficiency diseases?

Some people have a medical condition that makes it hard for them to absorb a certain vitamin or mineral. Other people eat such a small variety of foods that they do not get all the nutrients they need. But the people who are most likely to suffer from deficiency diseases are the millions of people throughout the world who are starving or who do not have enough money to eat a good diet. Even in rich countries, there are many people, especially those who are very old or very poor, who cannot afford to feed themselves properly.

Effects of deficiency diseases

Vitamins and minerals perform many different functions in the body. So, a deficiency disease usually affects the body in a number of different ways. The person's body does not work well and he or she often feels ill and weak. The skin, muscles, blood, or bones may be particularly affected.

Older people are more at risk of developing some deficiency diseases than younger people. As people get older, they need to make more effort to stay fit and healthy.

Storing Minerals and Vitamins

Your body stores some minerals and vitamins, especially the vitamins that are **soluble** in fats. Your **liver,** for example, can store enough vitamin D to last for two years.

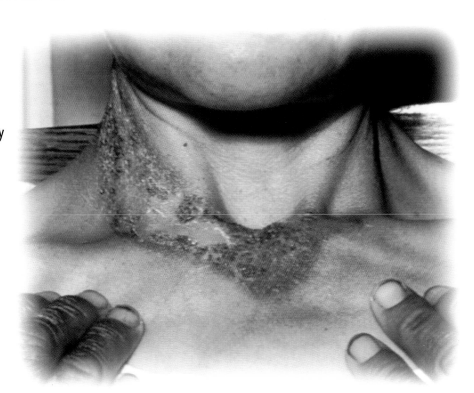

This person is suffering from pellagra, caused by a lack of the B vitamin, niacin. The skin around the neck has become sore and irritated.

Pellagra

Pellagra is caused by a lack of niacin and other B vitamins. It is common among people who eat mainly corn, since corn does not contain much niacin. People feel weak, but not hungry, and they suffer from indigestion and **diarrhea.** Their skin becomes irritated, dark, and scaly, especially where it is not protected from sunlight.

Beriberi

Beriberi is caused by a lack of the B vitamin thiamine. It used to be common in China, Japan, and other parts of Asia where people ate "polished" rice, which is rice that contains no thiamine. The name of the disease means "I cannot" in one of the languages of southern Asia. It describes how sufferers become too sick to do anything. Their legs become stiff, paralyzed, and painful. Today, thiamine is added to white rice, and the disease has become less common.

Other Vitamin Deficiencies

Too little vitamin A

A lack of vitamin A affects the nerve endings in the eyes that sense dim light. This makes it hard or impossible to see in the dark, a condition known as night blindness. A lack of vitamin A is also known to make it harder for your body to fight off diseases and can make you grow more slowly.

Not enough B vitamins

Because your body cannot store B vitamins, a shortage of them can affect your health after just a few months. In addition to causing beriberi and pellagra, a shortage of vitamin B_{12} or of folate can cause **anemia.** A person with anemia does not have enough healthy red blood **cells** to keep the cells supplied with oxygen. People with anemia feel tired and lacking in energy.

Too little vitamin C

A shortage of vitamin C can cause a lack of iron. In extreme cases, lack of vitamin C keeps the body from being able to heal. This condition is called scurvy. The small blood vessels that supply your cells become weak and blood spills out under the skin. It is particularly noticeable in the gums and mouth, which both become sore. The person's gums bleed and their teeth become loose.

Scientists use microscopes to check a blood sample to find out if a person has anemia. They count the number of healthy red blood cells in the sample.

Rickets is a disease that can make a person bowlegged. Children who lack vitamin D or calcium may develop rickets.

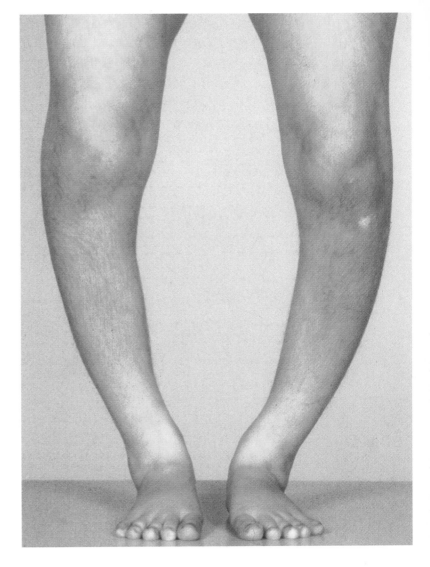

Too little vitamin D

Since vitamin D controls how much calcium your body absorbs and uses, a lack of vitamin D leads to a lack of calcium. Children need plenty of vitamin D and calcium because their bones are still growing. If they do not get enough, they may develop rickets. This means that their bones do not grow strong and straight.

Too little vitamin E

Your body stores vitamin E in the fat that lies under your skin. It is unlikely that your diet will lack vitamin E. The only people who are at risk are people whose bodies cannot absorb the vitamin and **premature** babies. Babies that are born early have very little body fat and very little stored vitamin E. Unless they are given extra vitamin E, they get anemia.

Too little vitamin K

A shortage of vitamin K means that the blood does not clot properly. So, if you cut yourself, the wound will bleed much more and for a longer time than it should. This deficiency is very unlikely to happen, however, because your body constantly makes vitamin K in your large intestine. A small number of newborn babies are short of the vitamin, so babies are usually given extra vitamin K as soon as they are born.

Mineral Deficiencies

Too little calcium

Children and young adults need to eat plenty of foods that contain calcium because it is good for your bones. Children who do not get enough calcium may develop rickets, a disease that makes people's leg bones bend outward. People who do not develop strong bones when they are young are also at risk of developing a condition called osteoporosis when they are older. People with this condition can break bones easily.

Too little salt

If you often get muscle cramps, you may be suffering from a lack of salt, particularly if the weather is hot or you often play sports that make you sweat. When you sweat, your body loses salt as well as water. You may feel thirsty, but you may not realize that you also have to replace the salt you have lost. Lack of salt can make you feel tired and sick as well.

Runners and other athletes drink special sports drinks that contain salt as well as water. These drinks replace the salt they lose through sweating.

Osteoporosis

Many older women suffer from osteoporosis. The people who have the condition have lost a lot of calcium in their bones and their bones have become very brittle, or easily breakable. Once the calcium has been lost, older people cannot replace it. Younger women can take steps to prevent osteoporosis. These include eating a balanced diet with plenty of calcium and vitamin D, exercising using weights, and leading a healthy lifestyle that includes no smoking or excessive alcohol use.

Too little potassium or magnesium

The people most likely to have a shortage of potassium or magnesium are those who are suffering from a disease called kwashiorkor, caused by a lack of **protein**. Diseases that cause severe and long-lasting **diarrhea** may also lead to a shortage of potassium or magnesium. If this happens, the person may have a heart attack and die.

Too little iron

A shortage of iron is one of the most common causes of **anemia**. Lack of iron means that the body cannot produce **hemoglobin** and so leads to a shortage of red blood **cells**. Not having enough red blood cells keeps cells in your body from getting all the **oxygen** they need.

Too little iodine

People who do not get enough iodine in their diet suffer from a disease of the **thyroid gland** known as goiter. The gland swells up, and the neck can become huge.

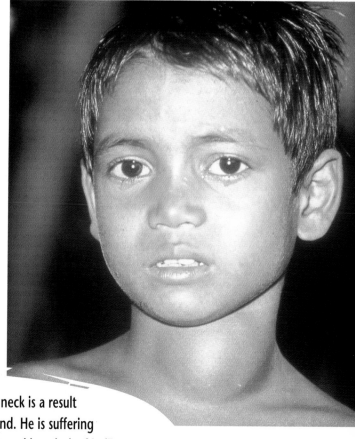

The swelling on this boy's neck is a result of an enlarged thyroid gland. He is suffering from goiter, a condition caused by a lack of iodine.

Healthy Eating

If you eat a diet containing a wide variety of foods, you should get all the vitamins and minerals you need. You also need to eat a balanced diet. The Food Guide Pyramid shows you how much you should eat of different kinds of food.

Bread, cereal, rice, and pasta

The foods in this group all contain a lot of **carbohydrates** and will keep your body supplied with **energy.** They are also rich in vitamins and minerals. Whole grain foods such as brown rice and whole wheat bread are especially good sources of B vitamins, vitamin E, and iron. You should eat six to eleven servings a day from this group.

Vegetables

Vegetables are rich in a wide variety of vitamins and minerals and in **fiber.** Your digestive system needs fiber in order to work correctly. You should eat three to five servings of vegetables every day.

Fruits

Fruits are an important source of carbohydrates. Like vegetables, they are high in fiber. Fruits are good sources of vitamins, especially A and C. Some fruits are also good sources of minerals. For example, bananas and dried figs are high in magnesium and potassium. You should eat two to four servings from this group every day.

Meat, poultry, fish, dry beans, eggs, and nuts

This group is rich in **protein.** Meat, poultry, fish, and eggs are animal proteins and are particularly rich in B vitamins and iron. Dry beans and nuts are vegetable proteins. They are also a good source of most B vitamins and a number of minerals. You should eat two to three servings from this group each day.

Milk, yogurt, and cheese

These foods provide proteins, **fats,** fat-**soluble** vitamins (A, D, E, and K), and many minerals, particularly calcium. It is recommended that you eat two to three servings from this group each day.

Fats, Oils, and Sweets

At the top of the pyramid are fats, oils, and sweets. We should not eat these foods often and only in small amounts. These foods include butter, potato chips, cookies, and chocolate.

The Food Guide Pyramid shown below was created to give you an idea of what to eat each day to maintain a healthful diet.

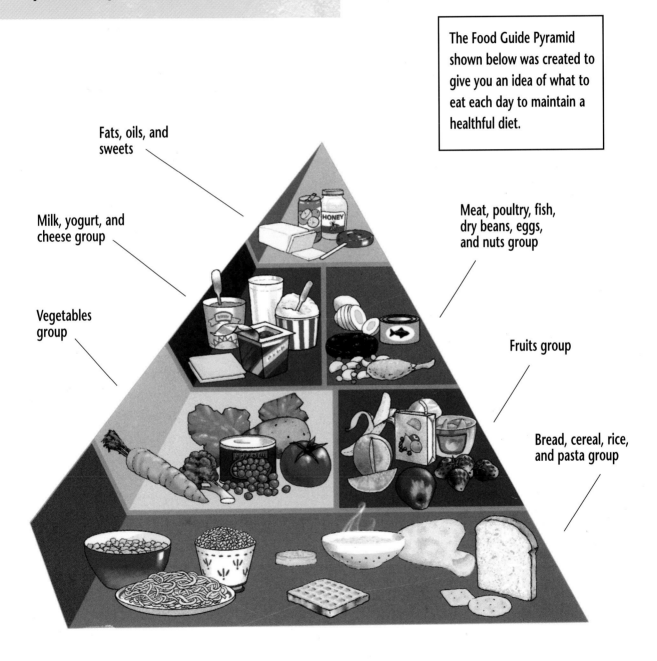

Fats, oils, and sweets

Milk, yogurt, and cheese group

Vegetables group

Meat, poultry, fish, dry beans, eggs, and nuts group

Fruits group

Bread, cereal, rice, and pasta group

Special Needs

While most people can get all the vitamins and minerals they need by eating a varied and balanced diet, some groups of people need to take extra vitamins or minerals. They can do this by choosing foods that are rich in the **nutrients** they need or by taking vitamin and mineral pills.

Vegans

Vegetarians eat dairy products, which help them get all the vitamins and minerals they need. But vegans do not eat any food that comes from animals. They may not get enough vitamin B_{12}, which is found mainly in meat, fish, eggs, and dairy products. Vegans may need to get this necessary vitamin in the form of a vitamin pill.

Pregnant women

When a woman is pregnant, her body gives some of the nutrients she takes in to the baby growing inside her. She has to make sure she eats enough for herself, too. She especially needs extra iron, calcium, and vitamins C and D so the baby can build strong bones and red blood

cells. Pregnant women are usually given extra folate, or folic acid, to protect their unborn babies from a condition called **spina bifida.** Pregnant women should avoid liver because it contains a lot of vitamin A. Too much vitamin A can cause **birth defects**. They should also avoid certain fish.

During pregnancy, women must eat food that contains plenty of vitamins and minerals and avoid eating liver and certain fish.

Babies and young children

Babies that breast-feed get all the nutrients they need from their mother's milk. Once they have stopped breast-feeding, however, it is important that they eat a healthful diet that includes all the vitamins they need, but not extra salt. Many babies and young children are given drops that contain extra vitamins A, C, and D.

Older people

As people grow older, they tend to eat less. They have to take extra care to make sure they are getting enough of all nutrients, including vitamins and minerals. Older people who do not go outside cannot make vitamin D from sunlight and may lack this vitamin so they should eat foods that provide vitamin D.

Athletes

Athletes are usually very careful about the food they eat and make sure their bodies are fit and healthy. However, if they take part in sports that make them sweat a lot for many hours, they have to drink extra liquid during the event. Special sports drinks contain extra salt to replace the salt lost in sweating.

This baby is learning to feed himself. Parents must make sure that the food their children eat is healthy. Many baby foods have vitamins and minerals added to them.

Nutritional Information

The two tables on this page show how much of some vitamins and minerals you should have every day. Most Americans eat a lot of salt (or sodium chloride). Too much sodium can lead to heart problems. The American Heart Association recommends that adults get no more than 0.11 ounces (3,000 milligrams) of sodium per day. One teaspoon of salt contains 0.08 ounces (2,300 milligrams) of sodium.

Recommended daily intakes of some vitamins

A microgram (abbreviated µg) is one millionth of a gram. A milligram (abbreviated mg) is one thousandth of a gram. Ten million micrograms and 10,000 milligrams are both equal to about 0.35 ounces.

Age	A (µg)	B$_6$ (mg)	B$_{12}$ (µg)	Folate (µg)	D (mg)	E (µg)
7–10	700	1.4	1.4	100	10	10
adult female	800	1.6	2.0	400	5	15
adult male	1,000	2.0	2.0	400	5	15

Recommended daily intakes of some minerals in milligrams (mg)

0.35 ounces = 10,000 milligrams

Age	Calcium	Iron	Zinc	Magnesium
7–10	800–1,200	10	10	170
adult female	1,000–1,500	10–15	12	280
adult male	1000	10	15	350

Smoking and Vitamin C

A study published in 2003 found that kids whose parents smoked cigarettes were likely to have lower levels of vitamin C in their bloodstreams than kids whose parents did not smoke. Children with parents who smoke should try to eat more vitamin-C foods, such as strawberries, broccoli, and potatoes.

This table shows how many milligrams (mg) of some vitamins and minerals are contained in 3.5 ounces (100 grams) of different foods.

Food (3.5 ounce portion)	Thiamine (mg)	Vitamin C (mg)	Calcium (mg)	Iron (mg)	Sodium (mg)
Spaghetti (boiled and unsalted)	0.01	0	7	0.50	0
Boiled rice	0.01	0	18	0.20	1
White bread	0.21	0	110	1.60	3
Cornflakes	1.00	0	15	6.70	1,110
Baked potato	0.37	14	11	0.70	12
Raw cabbage	0.15	49	52	0.70	5
Cucumber	0.03	2	18	0.30	3
Boiled spinach	0.06	6	150	1.70	16
Green peppers	0.08	128	6	1.20	4
Apples	0.03	6	4	0.10	3
Blueberries	0.05	13	6	4.80	6
Dates	0.07	1	230	3.90	10
Oranges	0.11	54	47	0.10	5
Strawberries	0.03	77	16	0.40	6
Baked beans	0.09	0	53	1.40	530
Bacon	0.43	0	12	1.50	2,020
Ground beef	0.05	0	18	3.10	320
Canned sardines	0.04	0	550	2.90	650
Whole milk	0.03	1	115	0.06	55
Cheddar cheese	0.03	0	720	0.30	670
Low-fat fruit yogurt	0.05	1	150	0.10	64
Chocolate	0.10	0	220	1.60	120
Chocolate cookies	0.03	0	110	1.70	160

Glossary

acid chemical compound that aids in digestion

amino acid smaller unit or building block of proteins. Different amino acids combine together to form a protein.

anemia medical condition in which a person does not have enough healthy red blood cells to keep his or her cells supplied with oxygen

antioxidant type of vitamin or substance believed to protect body cells from damage and aging

artery tube that carries blood from the heart to different parts of the body

bacteria microscopic living things. Some are helpful, like those in our intestines, but some can cause disease.

bile substance made in the liver that breaks up the fats in food

birth defect physical problem or condition present when a baby is born

bone marrow jellylike substance in the center of some bones where red and white blood cells are made

carbohydrate substance in food that the body uses to provide energy. Foods rich in carbohydrates include bread, rice, potatoes, and sugar.

carbon dioxide one of the gases in the air. Animals breathe out carbon dioxide.

cell smallest unit of a plant or animal

chemical reaction when two or more chemicals react together to produce a change

cholesterol fatty substance found in some foods and in most parts of your body, including the blood

chyme mushy liquid that passes from the stomach to the small intestine

deficiency disease disease caused by a lack of a certain vitamin or mineral

dentin thick, bone-like tissue that makes up most of a tooth

diarrhea condition in which the feces are loose and watery

dissolve break down or mix with a liquid so that the liquid is the same throughout

DNA substance that genes are made from

duodenum first part of the small intestine

element simple substance made up of only one kind of chemical

energy ability to do work or to make something happen

enzyme substance that helps a chemical reaction take place faster

esophagus   tube through which food travels from the mouth to the stomach

fat   substance found in a wide range of foods. The body can change fat into energy. Fat is stored by the body in a layer below the skin.

fatty acid   kind of acid found in animal fat and vegetable oils and fats

fiber   substance found in plants that cannot be digested by the human body

free radical   chemical that damages protein and DNA in the body's cells

genetic code   instructions that tell your cells what to do and how to make new cells

glucose   simple form of sugar that is broken down from carbohydrate food during digestion

glycogen   substance made by different glands in the body that affects or controls certain organs, cells, or tissues

hemoglobin   chemical in your red blood cells that carries oxygen

hormone   substance made by different glands in the body that affects or controls certain organs, cells, or tissues

liver   organ in the body that plays a role in digestion. It makes bile and helps clean the blood. People also eat beef and chicken livers, which are a rich source of protein, vitamins, and minerals.

molecule   smallest unit into which a substance can be divided and still have the properties of that substance

nutrient   substance found in foods that help the body grow and stay healthy. Proteins, carbohydrates, fats, vitamins, and minerals are all nutrients.

organ   body part that has a particular job to do. An eye is an example of an organ.

ovary   part of a woman's body where eggs are produced. Women have two ovaries.

oxygen   gas present in the air and used by the body. Oxygen is one of the most common elements and is used by the body to make amino acids.

pharynx   back of the throat

premature   happening too soon. A premature baby is one that is born before it is due.

protein   complex chemical that the body needs to grow and repair cells

puberty   time of life when a child's body develops into an adult's body

saliva   watery liquid made by glands in the mouth and the inside of the cheeks

soluble   able to dissolve in liquid

spina bifida   inherited disease that affects the spine

starch   carbohydrates stored in plants

stroke   sudden change in blood supply to the brain that can cause loss of movement in parts of the body

thyroid gland   gland that affects growth and the production of energy and waste in the body

trace element   mineral that is important for health but is only needed in very small amounts

villus   tiny, fingerlike extension in the small intestine through which digested food and water are absorbed. More than one villus are called villi.

virus   tiny, nonliving thing inside your body that can make you sick

Further Reading

Dalton, Cindy Devine. *Love My Vitamins.* Vero Beach, Fla.: Rourke
    Publishing, 2000.

D'Amico, Joan, and Karen Eich Drummond. *The Healthy Body Cookbook.*
    Hoboken, N.J.: John Wiley & Sons, 1999.

Douglas, Ann, and Julie Douglas. *Body Talk: The Straight Facts on Fitness,
    Nutrition and Feeling Great about Yourself.* Toronto, Ontario,
    Canada: Maple Tree Press, 2002.

Healthy Kids Challenge Staff. *Simple Recipes, Healthy Meals.*
    Birmingham, Ala.: Oxmoor House, 2001.

Kalbacken, Joan. *The Food Pyramid.* Danbury, Conn.: Children's Press,
    1998.

Kalbacken, Joan. *Vitamins and Minerals.* Danbury, Conn.: Children's Press,
    1998.

Petrie, Kristin. *Vitamins Are Vital.* Edina, Minn.: ABDO Publishing, 2003.

Royston, Angela. *Eating and Digestion.* Chicago: Heinemann Library,
    1998.

Weintraub, Aileen. *Everything You Need to Know about Eating Smart.* New
    York: Rosen Publishing, 2000.

Westcott, Patsy. *Diet and Nutrition.* Austin, Tex.: Raintree Publishers,
    2000.

Index